My Daddy is a Window Cleaner

by ryan kirby

My daddy is a window cleaner,
He even cleans castles sometimes,
It is not an easy job to have,
But he's always home by bedtime,

To get to daddy's castle clean,
there's lots of very long roads,
It's good he didn't have to walk,
The driveway's full of toads!

The gigantic castle is surrounded by a very deep moat, its vile!
He's careful and must watch his step,
So he doesn't swim with a crocodile,

Imagine working in the rain,
My daddy has to sometimes,
It makes him very very wet,
But the sun will shine by lunchtime,

Daddy had to turn the power off to the bouncy castle, Because the sparrows kept bouncing too high And hitting all the windows

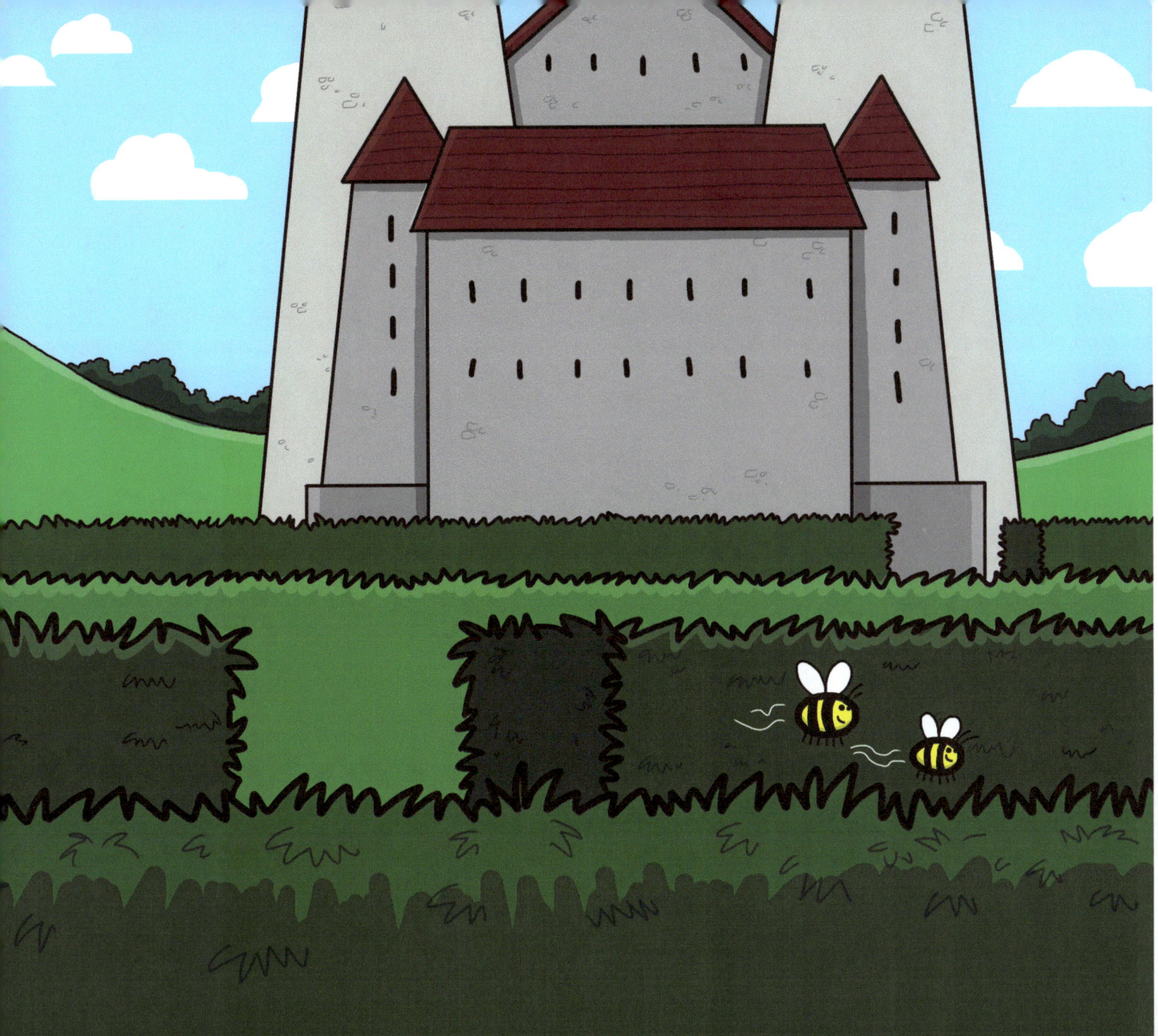

Around the castle is a beautiful maze,
It is really quite a sight,
But daddy finds it hard to see,
When he trips and takes a flight,

Another danger my daddy faces,
Is all the creepy crawlies,
Cleaning windows can be so scary
Avoiding spiders eating ice lollies,

astles are home to funny looking creatures,
                making funny noises,
     But most amusing of them all,
     Are hippos playing cowboys,

Some castle windows are 100 miles high,
you cant see them from the ground,
Daddy cleans upon a ladder,
Being careful not to fall inbound,

Daddy is always moaning,
about the job that is most dumb,
All of the bird's poo on the windows,
It's worse when they eat bubble gum!

Very very rarely daddy will
meet a badger or a fox,
It makes it much more funny when,
When they both are wearing crocs!

There're some very awkward windows to reach,
when you clean a castle,
To clean some, he has to climb a tree,
It really is a hassle,

And that was daddy's castle clean, all sparkling and finished.

Its bedtime now, my nightlight is aglow,
I can't stop yawning,
Can't wait until morning,
for the same again tomorrow.

The End

www.ingramcontent.com/pod-product-compliance
Lightning Source LLC
Chambersburg PA
CBHW041442010526
44118CB00003B/153